MW01234525

By Rust of Nail & Prick of Thorn

By Rust of Nail & Prick of Thorn
The Theory & Practice of Effective Home Warding

Althaea Sebastiani

©2017 Althaea Sebastiani

All rights reserved. This book or parts thereof
may not be reproduced in any form, stored in
any retrieval system, or transmitted in any
form by any means—electronic, mechanical,
photocopy, recording, or otherwise—without
prior written permission of the publisher, except
as provided by United States of America
copyright law. For permission requests, contact
the publisher at info@ladyalthaea.com
Reviewers may quote brief passages.

Second Edition

ISBN:
Print 9798690534851
ebook 9781370042876

This book was made possible thanks to The Winding Way witches. No words can accurately express my appreciation for your continued support and encouragement.

Table of Contents

Foreword to the Second Edition

Like with so many things in life, the creation of this small book was an accident. The intention was to produce a quick article covering the basics of home warding. But, of course, intention cannot compare to action and the impact of those actions. That "quick" article quickly reached five-thousand words.

"Reel it in or keep going and see what happens?" I asked the witches who supported my burgeoning work as a professional writer. Unrepentant enablers, "Write!" they said. And so I did.

In the three years since this small book was published, the words have continued to flow. The warm reception it received (and continues to receive) surprised and encouraged me. Soon after, my first course—and the most important thing I've written to date—*Be a Local Witch* would be born. And still the words would flow.

This small, accidental book played such an important part in bolstering my confidence in writing more formally on witchcraft and Paganism. It would be the reason I could retire from freelance writing and commit full-time to working as a spirit worker and writer, leading to the creation of now 12 courses, my book *Paganism for Beginners*, and more books to come. I continue to be grateful for all this small book has made possible.

This second edition does contain some minor changes from the first edition, mainly, some expansion and tightening of language throughout the book for clarity. This edition, thanks to being solely available as a paperback, also features a glossary and index.

As with all of my writing, this book was never meant to coddle or give you all the answers but, rather, to encourage you to experiment within your practice, to be innovative, to learn through doing and, thus, further discover how capable you are as a witch. And you are so very capable.

May this pocket guide to effective home warding serve you well.

Althaea
October, 2020

Prelude

In reading through this book, you will likely
notice a different approach to witchcraft than is
found in other books you've read. You will not
find copious lists of correspondences nor
scripted magick devoid of explanation for you to
repeat. Nor will you find suggestions to call
upon Gods you don't know or to perform highly
generic spells for your specific needs. Rather,
the approach to witchcraft herein is much more
pragmatic and based on the simple goal of
encouraging you to be the most competent and
effective witch you can be.

A witch is someone who practices witchcraft
—*there are no other qualifiers.* And a competent
witch is someone who, after having learned the
basics, is capable of analyzing their unique
situation, determining how best to approach the
situation, and following through with
appropriate action supported by their own
abilities and the materials that they already
have on hand.

Remember, it's called witch**craft** not
witch*think*: the magick you work will always be
more effective than the magick you don't work.

It is my hope that this book encourages you
to be willing to act, to figure out how to solve

your problems, and to *do* the witchcraft. There is no need to stress about not having the right materials, that the moon isn't in the right phase, or that you just "aren't ready." You have everything you need, the moon is just fine, and you are ready just as you are. If you have a need for magick, then you are ready, right now, to use it for your benefit.

Witchcraft is inherently secular, able to be practiced within or without any religious context due to its own fluid nature. Should you choose to incorporate religion, *any* religion—not just Wicca and generic Paganism—that decision rests entirely on you. There is no judgment to be found here, merely the hope that you will choose to act when, before, you may have made excuses not to and that you walk your path with integrity and sincerity.

That said, to make the most of the information within this book, you should already have a good (if not firm) grip on the basics of witchcraft, that is, how to feel and move energy. These skills are critical for any sort of competency and to effectively use magick in any way. All other skills and abilities are based on these fundamentals. Step by step instructions for everything will not be included in this book, though for the purpose of being comprehensive,

basic steps for rendering an object an effectively
charged ward will be discussed.

If you take nothing else away from this book,
would that it be the willingness to act.

Introduction

Basic warding and protection magick are fundamental to the practice of witchcraft. Reasons for this are similar to why you would safeguard yourself in any other situation. You lock the doors to your home each night not because you think someone is going to break in but because it is a precautionary measure, serving to keep out unwanted guests—be they human or animal (I'm looking at you raccoons) —and can even prevent damage to your home in the event of severe weather. Likewise, you safeguard your physical health by washing your hands, wearing a seat belt, and getting vaccinated. In this way, warding is a combination of magickal prophylactic and basic magickal hygiene. It is a preventative means of magickally guarding your spiritual health— helping to prevent situations that would adversely affect you—and helping to better keep you at the top of your game.

What is Warding?

Warding is a practical magickal means of protecting and securing a person or place. The exact procedure and materials can range from complex to deceptively simple. However, it's important to remember that, with magick, the power lays not within the objects or the words, but within the witch and their ability to tap into the wild and ancient forces that exist within and without us all. For that reason, very ordinary objects can be rendered *very* powerful wards.

When done effectively, warding can keep your home protected from all outside influence—the exception, here, being unless you (or someone with whom you share your home) bring that influence into the warded dwelling, and outside influences can very easily be brought into your home by your own doing, however unconsciously.

Note that warding is not an action that renders the interior of your home cleansed and/or purified, rather, it is more so a means of locking the house down: shutting all the entrances and locking them, thereby keeping what's out *out* and what's in *in*. This is a very important point to keep in mind should you find yourself subject to a curse or spirit attack and needing to secure your home as part of the process. In such an instance, warding your home would be the final step, with purification of yourself, warding yourself, and cleansing your home occurring first.

The exact details of what is allowed to pass through your wards can be laid out as part of the creation and setting of your wards. In this way, warding does not interfere with your spell casting nor does it interfere with the travel and tasks of any spirit allies, the fetch, or familiars, and it does not interfere with your ability to worship or work with any deities. In the case of worship of or work done with a deity, if you regularly do so at a shrine (dedicated physical space that has been devoted to that particular deity) or an altar (purposely constructed temporary physical space that serves as a portal between the worlds through which energies and entities may be called forth or sent through) then that deity already has a free pass on access to your home as that shrine is Theirs and that altar is a doorway through which They may enter *because it was created for Their use.*

Most means of warding utilize physical objects as anchor points for energy. Those physical objects bear the same name as the action they take and the same name as any purely energetic barriers that may be constructed to safeguard your home: wards.

Part One
Theory

The simplest way to think of what warding is, regarding your home, is that it is merely shutting a door and locking it against intruders. And for the witch who is regularly practicing magick, there are a surprising number of things that are best locked out of your home, things that will interfere with your witchcraft (not to mention life in general), and that can easily go unnoticed.

What do You Ward Against?

For the witch, warding the home can be a fairly casual practice. It doesn't take much to throw up a good ward that will serve to keep your home secure from unwanted energy and entities. This isn't a practice done because of some paranoia-based idea that there are people out to get you. Rather, warding is basic magickal hygiene, a form of prevention that also provides you with a continuous opportunity to practice your witch skills, thereby strengthening your power.

It is important to note that most people who practice magick and/or witchcraft will never be cursed in their lives. While that in itself is a topic for another time, it comes down to two simple points:

• most magick practitioners don't have the skill to effectively curse, regardless of personal assessment of their capabilities
• those that do have the skill to effectively curse more likely than not do not know you, do

not care about you, and/or don't see you as being worth the effort and consequences of cursing.

Cursing is serious business. Those who have the ability to effectively curse are not going to curse just because they can. You would really need to anger, offend, or harm them to an extent that they deem cursing to be the best response. In which case: up your warding, cleanse your home and self, work your trusty protection magick, and continuously check in on your wards till the threat has passed (which you can determine through divination and through your familiars).

What is being warded against, exactly, will differ from witch to witch, simply due to the type of magick they work, the location of their home (there may be natural traits to the landscape that afford protection or which may even serve to increase the need for good warding, such as being near a crossroads), who they share their home with, and what is or is not naturally attracted to that witch (because we all attract things to us, be they certain energies or types of spirits).

In general, there are three things that you can and may want to ward your home against:

- disruptive energy
- intrusion
- transient Spirits

Disruptive Energy

No, we're not talking about the highly ambiguous, utterly erroneous, and positively nonexistent "negative energy" here (pun intended). Energy is not positive, it is not negative, it just *is*. Any demarcation of energy (i.e., protective energy, healing energy, etc.) comes through application and, as such, is a distinction that exists solely on the mental plane for the purpose of functionality.

In other words, it's more effective for us to use energy if we envision it divided as such even if the reality doesn't support that division. However, we can and do program objects to behave in a way that uses energy to a specific end, e.g., making a ward and charging it to protect against psychic spying. The energy used to accomplish that end is the same as would be used to accomplish any other magickal goal, but the manner in which that ward is constructed causes it to behave in a particular way. Its construction causes it to use the energy in a specific manner to accomplish its specific job—there is nothing inherent to the energy used that causes the ward to behave a certain way.

This does not negate the truth that certain objects, herbs, stones, etc. are more appropriately put to specific uses and not to other uses (e.g., chamomile is used in love magick, while smoky quartz is an energy sink, and coyote teeth can help you get through tricky situations). In these instances, their energy is more appropriately suited to that use because the energy is being filtered through that physical form in the same way as how your personality is not the same expression as your soul/spirit. The one is filtered through physicality, which absolutely changes the way that it manifests. To put it another way, the spirit who was Gandhi could very easily reincarnate as a luchador with a gluten intolerance, and while bergamot is useful for financial prosperity it is not useful for spirit travel.

For the purpose of warding, disruptive energy includes all energy that you have not deliberately invited into your home and that can —and does—affect you, your family/housemates, and your spell work. It is not energy that is purposely directed at you (see the next point, *Intrusion*,) rather it naturally finds its way into your home or accumulates as a result of activities that occur within close proximity to your home.

It's important to note that disruptive energy can accumulate due to occurrences *within* your home, as well. However, this is not something you can ward against but it is something for which you can effectively cleanse and take practical measures. Some examples of these types of occurrences include arguments, miasma, and things that can cause miasma for you (more on this in the next section, *What You Cannot Ward Against*).

Homes that are particularly subject to disruptive energy are located within or near the following areas:

• an apartment building, housing complex, dormitory, or other type of structure that many people live in, either independently or as roommates, and where the inhabitants frequently change out; or a building that has been converted from a multi-housing unit, hotel, hospital, etc. into a single-family unit

- densely populated areas or where a neighbor's home is extremely close by (e.g., townhouses, duplexes, or houses with very narrow side yards)
- near a crossroads, especially a busy or old but still in use crossroads
- near a busy road
- near to a public space, especially if it is frequently in use, such as a park or library

Intrusion

Intrusion is consciously directed energy or magickal/psychic attention from others, whereas disruptive energy is general and not consciously directed at you nor purposely seeking to cause havoc in your life. However, it is important to note that someone does not have to practice magick (in any way) to be able to psychically intrude on another. We all know that person who, despite not being a witch, is quite adept at throwing the evil eye. And many of us have that person in our lives whom we can easily "check in with" mentally, and know that they're okay and to whom we can even convey simple messages.

For someone proficiently skilled (whether they be a conscious magick practitioner or not,) forming a psychic connection with someone in order to attempt to influence or intrude upon their life really isn't that difficult. A screen name and social media avatar can be sufficient for someone to get a lock on you and attempt to throw some magickal shade your way. Luckily, with such a tenuous connection, this sort of link and energy exchange are easily warded against using some of the techniques covered later in this book.

Here are the three primary ways that conscious magickal intrusion occurs:

Psychic Spying

This can take numerous forms, in application, but the end result is the same: someone is using psychic abilities in order to forge a link with you and gain information. That information can be as seemingly benign as how you're feeling or whether you're at home. But it can be much more malicious, such as identifying emotional weak points, testing your magickal shielding (i.e., your home and personal warding,) or confirming whether you've noticed the preliminary effects of a curse.

Curses

This is the most blatant way that someone can magickally intrude in your life. A curse is any sort of consciously directed, unwanted energy that has been sent your way specifically for the purpose of causing mischief and mayhem. This includes being overlooked, the evil eye, and more ritualistically complicated acts of magick. It bears repeating: just because you practice magick/witchcraft does not mean that you are now, will be, or have ever been cursed. Refer to the section *What Does One Ward Against?* for further on this.

Unwanted Magick & Blessings

This applies primarily to the magickal and new age communities as they overlap with the Pagan and witchcraft communities, where it has become common practice to routinely bless someone, "light a candle" for them, and otherwise consciously direct energy at them without that individual's permission—

sometimes to the extent that various deities are called in to further assist (not that this guarantees that deity would do as requested, the Gods are autonomous and subject to our will or Will). Considering how such action was generally considered unethical a decade ago (oh, the heated online debates about not working healing magick without someone's permission) it is interesting to note this change. For the witch who takes effort to control the energy within their life as much as is possible, such deliberate action is disrespectful, intrusive, unwanted, and just another hassle that need be dealt with and diffused.

Transient Spirits

Similar to disruptive energy, transient spirits find their way into your home unbidden and typically leave on their own. Sometimes, they may stick around for a while if they find you interesting. More often than not, though, you may never be aware of these spirits as they pass through so quickly. Others may enjoy staring at you while you sleep, peeking around corners, or crawling across the ceiling during their brief visits. At best, these spirits do little more than set your hair on end, but there are always those spirits whose presence causes disruption, either deliberately or just as a natural consequence of them being there.

For example, a sudden stretch of cups falling off of counters or framed pictures on the wall refusing to hang straight can indicate a sudden new spirit making its presence known. However, it could even be the resident spirits in your home reacting adversely to this transient spirit, alerting you to the new comer, acting out, or working to drive this spirit from your home. Other signs of a transient spirit could include a general feeling of unease in your home, shorter tempers, difficulty sleeping, and a lack of energy. You may also just *know* that there's somebody extra within your home, feeling as if you're being watched or that something just isn't quite right. In all instances, divination can confirm or point out the real culprit.

Of course, sometimes a spirit will purposely seek you out, either because you are naturally attractive to it, you've done and/or are doing something that attracts it, or someone has sent that spirit to you. However, much like cursing, this is not as common as the internet would have you believe. Just because you practice magick/witchcraft does not mean that spirits are attracted to you. It certainly doesn't mean that "Evil Spirits" are after you.

The exception to this, of course, is the fact that working magick, consciously altering the energy currents about you, does create ripples. These ripples can be and are noticed by spirits. But there are more spirits with disputable sentience than not and it is these lower type spirits that you will encounter most often. These types of spirits are frequently parasitic or scavengers and have come to feed because you're leaking energy, being sloppy with your magick, or because you naturally attract them. While they can be troublesome if left unchecked, these spirits are generally easily warded against (prevention) and banished (remedy).

***

In looking at the types of things that you would ward your home against, it's important to note that psychic/magickal means are most effective against psychic/magickal threats. Likewise, physical means are most effective against physical threats. It's not enough to simply do something to solve the problem, the action must make sense per the goal and that goal be clear.

It is for similar reasons why blanket "protection magick" for your home or an individual is often ineffective. *The focus is too general.* The energetic net is cast too wide and so it is thin, rendering that spell ineffective even against matters it would have otherwise been effective against. A single spell cannot cover more than one focus and have any chance of being successful. You must work specific magick if you want specific results.

For this reason, when you ward your home, it's important to place *many* wards as:

- there is a lot to be warded against
- even the smallest home has at least a dozen entry points (i.e., doors, windows, vents, exhaust pipes, cable inlets, etc.)
- depending on the type of ward, it may wear out and need recharging or replacing, or the ward may even need to be emptied

Having multiple wards provides back up and continuous coverage against a variety of potential hazards. It is the only way to ensure

that you have significant and potent protection
in the event that a ward becomes compromised.
It's also the only way to effectively protect your
home against a variety of potential psychic and
magickal threats.

What You Cannot Ward Against

As much as we may want to lock our homes
down tight, there are some things that cannot be
blocked or prevented by putting up wards.

That Which you have Already Invited in

No, this isn't like the whole Hollywood vampire
thing. Rather, this is an acknowledgment that if
your actions are serving to bring a thing into
your home or are serving to attach a thing to
you (so that you would inadvertently carry it in,)
then you can't ward against that. This thing
needs to be dealt with in another manner. What
kind of *thing* are we talking about? This could
be anything from the consequences of bad
choices (which may be tempting to, in the
moment, label as "bad luck,") to a connection

between you and another person that enables them to psychically spy on you.

This can be difficult to determine as the cause for current troublesome situations as it requires a bit of objectivity—which can be difficult to come by when stressed or frustrated. Regardless, it is only through a change in behavior (mundane action) that this cause can be remedied. This may mean finally cutting abusive people out of your life, learning to pay better attention to your finances, or even arguing less with strangers on the internet. An exception to this are pesky low-level parasitic spirits, which will attach to you and can, thus, overcome your home warding. Such a situation must be addressed specifically and will require follow up with a cleansing of the place where the removal of the spirit occurs and then tightening of that individual's personal and home wards (and likely some changes to personal habits and actions to prevent further problems).

Miasma

Given the nature of what miasma (ritual pollution) is, this should be a fairly obvious point. However, it has been repeatedly demonstrated that there is a general lack of understanding (or willingness to understand) this concept, so it warrants mentioning. Miasma is consequential energy that happens in life due to specific events, much like karma. For this reason, you cannot *prevent* miasma—you can only avoid miasmic situations and/or people and remedy it once you are in a state of miasma (again, much like how one avoids accumulating karma or remedies accumulated karma through another incarnation). This is done by abstaining from (unnecessary) activities that cause miasma and regular purification.

Generally, miasma inducing activities include anything that deals with crossing liminal spaces or dealing with the Underworld. This includes some fairly common acts of witchcraft, as well as some pretty ordinary occurrence in life, such as sex, marriage, a death in the family, and even illness. In addition to abstaining from miasma inducing activities (as much as is feasible), miasma can also be prevented by avoiding people and places that are currently in a miasmic state. Because miasma is not a permanent condition, it frequently remedies itself but sometimes ritual purification is useful to speed things up. This can be as simple as maintaining healthy boundaries in your life, turning the news off after you've already gotten the run down on current events, not reading books or watching movies that are emotionally upsetting or which stand in direct opposition to the values and virtues in which you are trying to live your life (because doing so isn't a challenge that strengthens you, rather, it distracts and makes the way harder).

It's also important to note, that what is miasmic to one person isn't necessarily miasmic to someone else. What is or is not miasmic can be cultural and can be specific to what gods you surround yourself with (or Who surround you). Miasma is also a natural and unavoidable consequence of very normal and human experiences. While it does cause spiritual complications (such as making it more difficult to engage deities and certain spirits) it can be remedied through ritual purification or time— which can be the only remedy with some sources of miasma, such as illness.

Deities

There is a reason why, in the world of spirits, humans have historically regarded gods and goddesses with extra measure. Regardless of whether or not you feel that deities are worthy of worship, it cannot be argued that They do not possess considerable power. Where other spirits' influence can be abated within our lives and their presence banished, the Gods, however, are less inclined to be swayed by human efforts to control Them. For this reason, even a home that is warded tightly and impenetrable to other spirits can be easily accessed by a deity Who chooses to do so. This is part of Their nature; we are fortunate that most deities choose to ignore us, individually (collectively is another matter), having Their own agenda and preoccupations.

Benefits of Warding

Warding your home affords numerous benefits, especially if you regularly cast spells, perform divination, and/or engage with spirits. Some benefits will present themselves daily, while others you may never consciously notice. However, not noticing your wards in action is often a good thing: it means they're working as they should and allowing you to carry on with your life and witchcraft uninterrupted.

At the most practical, warding your home gives the personal wards you carry on your person, or wear as periapt, a chance to rest and recharge, as they aren't needed as heavily, if at all. This allows these personal wards to be subjected to less wear and tear, enabling them to last longer and to more continuously perform at their peak. Obviously, this is a very good thing as you will need to replace or recharge them less often, freeing up your time for other, more pressing magickal needs.

Another benefit is that warding better regulates the energetic feel within your home. By preventing unwanted energies and transient spirits from entering your home, the overall energetic feel will be more stable. This facilitates strengthening feelings of security and safety that we naturally associate with home and being at home. Individuals who frequently experience nightmares may find some relief as a result of more stable energy within the home and otherwise jumpy house spirits may become noticeably calmer, too.

As warding reduces the amount of energetic "noise" for you to filter out, you may experience more sensitive psychic awareness. This is useful as you'll be more naturally aware of things that require your attention, such as situations with family members who are not home, to expect a visitor shortly, previously unknown health concerns in your own body, or messages from resident spirits and/or deities to Whom you have ties. In needing to filter out less energetic noise, you also benefit from a cleaner working space within which to work your magick, free of immediate influence and distraction.

A common complaint that many of us face, especially when trying to better incorporate witchcraft into our lives, is identifying practical ways to actually practice witchcraft on a regular basis. Once you get past the stage where you're casting a spell a night for every little thing you can think of, coming up with ideas for what to do, what sort of magick to work (especially magick that doesn't involve candles) can seem difficult and leave you feeling without direction. This makes warding your home especially useful as it affords continuous opportunities to practice witchcraft. And that continuous practicing helps to make you a better witch: stronger, more capable, and more aware.

Your awareness, specifically, becomes stronger through maintaining your wards. Maintenance involves regularly (weekly to monthly) checking your wards. Are they tired, full, or dead? Have they been tampered with or have they stopped something? This requires the development and strengthening of your psychic skills in order to be able to feel any changes within the ward and to recognize the difference between a properly functioning ward and one that is in need of charging, emptying, or replacing. In addition to the maintenance of your wards, their construction and any resulting divination and spell work necessary to handle any threat that may have been stopped provides you with ample opportunity to strengthen your abilities and can become the framework for a consistent witchcraft practice.

Caveat Regarding Warding Your Home Too Tightly

While light warding throughout your home is a good standard preventative measure, warding your home as tightly as you can cast should be left as a temporary reactive measure. In instances where you are under psychic, emotional, or mental attack, heavy warding *as supplement* to taking direct physical action is highly recommended. In this way, heavy warding enables you to more effectively cope and to take action to stop the attack. How long this heavier warding is maintained will vary as it is entirely dependent upon the specific situation.

For example, if you have a family member who isn't respecting your boundaries and autonomy as an adult, heavy warding to keep them from weighing so heavily on your mind, influencing your dreams, and calling you nightly to question your life choices can help give you some breathing space. Maintaining these wards for a week may be all that is necessary to help you gain ground in the discussion (i.e., get them to respect your choices), redirect their misspent focus (when was the last time they checked in on your siblings?), or to draw a hard line and tell them to leave you alone (and have them follow through on that).

But, for everyday purposes, sealing your home as tightly as you can just isn't necessary. Not only is it generally overkill for any energy or spirits you may encounter, it can also disrupt your ability to handle naturally fluctuating energies and low-level spirits on your own. In other words, it's easy to become too reliant on your wards, forfeiting your own capability and competence as a witch. Plus, it's too easy to fall into thinking that you need your wards or something catastrophic will happen. This just isn't the case. You absolutely can sleep in an unwarded home that lays at a busy crossroad on any of the nights when spirit travel is heightened and not experience the slightest disturbance. Remember, light warding is a healthy preventative measure, but heavily warding your home is a reactive measure—it's the big guns you pull out when a situation warrants such.

And, of course, while we are speaking of caveats... magickally warding your home is not an excuse to be stupid. It does not mean you can forego common sense measures such as not locking your doors and windows at night or when you leave the house. Too often, such sloppiness is taken as a challenge by the universe—do not welcome such challenges into your life if you can help it.

Part Two
Putting it into Practice

Creating wards and laying them throughout your home is a relatively simple process. Extremely effective wards can be made from materials you already own and you can easily ward your entire home within an hour. Beginning by first laying wards at the primary entry points of your home and then increasing the number of wards to cover other areas of your home and yard, over time, will provide you with the most successful results, as well as stronger warding.

Simple Wards for Your Home

Regardless of your approach and the number of wards you choose to lay initially, constructing your wards and setting them in place is not something that should be stressed or agonized over. It is far more important that a ward be created and put in place than it is that your ward looks a certain way or be made from certain specific materials. Focus on working with what you've got rather than worrying about how your magick would be "better" if you only had x, y, and z and you will become a better witch simply because you are actually practicing witchcraft and not just thinking about how you *should* be practicing witchcraft.

To further support this no-excuses approach to witchcraft, we're going to break down a selection of nine different ways that you can ward your home right now. These are simple means that you can use to shut that entry point into your home and create the lock that is your ward. Each of these means relies upon a physical object as an anchor point for the energy, even if that means in itself isn't physical. That physical object, however, is the focal point and is necessary for more consistent warding that requires less maintenance and attention. We'll look at a few purely energetic means of warding later on in *Emergency Warding: When You Have no Tools and Need to Ward Now.*

In the next section, we'll go over constructing your wards, how to charge them, and then the most effective locations to place them.

Charms

While the word *charm* originally meant an incantation, song, or verse that was recited as a spell, it has come to also refer to objects and acts that are employed as part of a spell or act of magick. This use as referring to objects is commonly used throughout contemporary witchcraft and so, for the purpose of clarity, that is the use employed explicitly herein. Per that use, then, a charm is an object that is deliberately constructed or modified so as to perform a magickal function. Charms are very versatile so that function could be anything, from protecting a pregnancy to healing a cold to attracting a new sexual partner. These objects may be created, such as in the case of a witch bottle which is made from a number of objects and materials, or it could be an object used as is and merely charged, such as with a holey stone.

Charms differ from tools in that, while they both affect the energy currents about them, tools do so actively, whereas charms do so passively. This is a basic mechanical difference but there are also other differences in application (e.g., tools are frequently used within a religious context when working with deities and other spirits, while charms are relegated to more folksy usage, being a standard component of folk magic practices) but this distinction is more than sufficient for the purposes of this book. Tools are also better suited for a quick, short-term effect (think a burst of energy) while charms are better suited for a slow, sustained effect (think radiating energy).

A charm can be crafted from anything. Truly anything. There are a few traditional charms that are made from specific ingredients, but their creation can be altered based upon what items you have access to. A perfect example of this is the witch bottle. While originally employed as a counter-curse, witch bottles make excellent wards operating as decoys or spirit traps.

The construction is the same: fill a jar or bottle with sharp bits of metal and personal items (such as urine, finger nail clippings, hair, few drops of blood, etc.). For a decoy to attract ill intent being hurtled your way, there is little more that need be added, however, you can also place additional items within to serve that counter-curse function, such as rusty metal, shards of broken glass or mirror, cactus spines, dead insects, or poisonous plants. Please note that if you have qualms with cursing, then counter-cursing should be avoided. It's a means of sending back the curse with an extra kick in the ass to let the person know to knock it off because you have teeth you aren't afraid to use. Please also note that a witch bottle serving as a decoy should be placed *outside* your home. This type of ward will eventually need to be disposed of and replaced. Bury or burn the old jar, being sure that all remains are off your property (burning a witch bottle is traditional, however, it is **ill advised**. But should you decide to burn your witch bottle anyway, even though I'm asking you nicely not do so, **please** do not be anywhere near the bottle as it sits in the fire. The chances of it exploding are high and you do not need to be showered in burning hot urine, shards of glass, and rusty metal. Please be safe).

For a spirit trap, the bottle should be placed near an entry point to your home. Additional items that you could add should have the intention of catching and keeping, so poisonous plants and dead insects won't be so effective as many seeds from specifically chosen plants or many extra pins, needles, rusty nails, and screws. This type of ward quite literally traps unwanted spirits inside of it. As such, it requires periodic checking, making sure that it isn't full and in need of disposal and replacing.

How do you know if it's full? Approach the bottle slowly, extending your witch senses and awareness about the bottle. Without touching the bottle, move your hand about it, feeling the air. You may notice a heaviness, like moving your hand through murky water. You may simply know that something (Someone?) is in there, either through clairsentience, well-developed awareness, or because the spirit is outraged and you can feel that anger. As for disposal: similar to a witch bottle used as a decoy, bury or burn. Lore tells us that if the bottle should pop when burning, it is a sign that there was indeed a spirit caught. Please note that *great* care should be taken, should you choose to burn the bottle, as the likelihood of it exploding and spraying hot urine and rusty bits of metal is high. Remember: common sense does not go out the window just because you're working magick.

Another traditional charm that works beautifully as a ward is a few rowan twigs bound in red thread. This same construction can be applied to other plants to make similar wards, such as wreaths or small bundles of thorns and brambles (similar to a witch's whisk, but it won't be burned, just placed), crossed and bound thorns or brambles, and braids of witch grass (which also work *beautifully* when burned to counter curses, cleanse your home, and otherwise banish unwanted spirits and energy).

Red thread alone works well as a ward, especially if knots are tied into it as part of the charging process. This thread can then easily (and inconspicuously) be tucked above doors and windows, tucked into molding about doors, or used as part of the construction of more complex wards.

The ubiquitous herbal charm bags are a relatively simple ward to create. All you need is a square of fabric (at least 3" long on each side,) and about a teaspoon's worth of herb matter—dried or fresh herbs are fine. Alternately, you can fashion a small drawstring bag, use a no longer needed baby sock, or empty and refill a paper tea bag in place of a square of fabric. All of these (as well as other creative options you may think of) can and do work just as effectively; you may choose to draw or embroider appropriate sigils onto the bag or select the color of the bag and thread per appropriate correspondence.

In addition to herbs and plant matter specifically chosen per their suitability for warding and protection, other items can be added to the charm bag. Items such as stones, small metal charms, spell remnants, zoological remains (i.e., bones, dried and preserved organs, claws, teeth, bits of fur, etc.), and a piece of paper with written instructions outlining the wards specific function (i.e., prevent psychic spying, to disallow psychic entry from those who would cause confusion and distress, etc.) are very much appropriate and potent.

After charging, these charm bags can be tucked into walls, crawlspaces, behind plants near entry ways, within cupboards, tucked behind mirrors and paintings, set on windowsills, hung in corners of entry ways, or placed beneath mattresses.

Chimes & Mobiles

Many wards, especially ones that are made and not wholly natural, could accurately be termed charms; chimes and mobiles are no exceptions. However, as they are often pre-made and enjoy a distinctly non-magickal use, they do warrant their own distinction.

Any wind chime or mobile can be charged and rendered a ward for your home or garden. Note that natural materials (i.e., wood, bamboo, metal, bones, shells, etc.) tend to more easily hold onto a magickal charge compared to synthetic materials. That is not to say that synthetic materials cannot be used, rather, there is something about materials such as plastic and glass that causes the charge to more readily dissipate.

Wards work by function of the energy stored within them, much like a battery. Unless there is a natural source of energy which they are programmed to use to replenish the energy used to do their job or a spirit is set to watch and replenish them, your wards will need to be touched up and recharged from time to time. So, expect your wards of synthetic materials to require more consistent maintenance; a bi-monthly or even weekly recharging may be necessary.

Wind chimes tend to be a polarizing object in general: many people love them, while others find them intolerable. Nonetheless, and maybe skip over the next two paragraphs if you fall into the latter party, chimes make very good wards due to their basic construction, ease of availability, and how inconspicuous they are (despite the noise) thanks to how common they are. Even hanging wind chimes indoors is not so out of the ordinary as to raise suspicion or demand inquiry. If anything, guests will just think you quirky—which, given your practice of witchcraft, you probably are. So, this only makes your indoor wind chimes all the more inconspicuous.

The sound produced by the wind chimes—regardless whether they are made of metal, bamboo, glass, or ceramic—has the effect of clearing the air. Bells are notorious for their use in dispelling unwanted energies, spirits, and even the fey; this quality is similarly possessed by wind chimes.

Mobiles can also be purchased pre-made, but they are an object that lends themselves well to purposeful creation. A bit of jute twine and a few pretty stones, shells, or bones suspended from a sturdy branch can easily be assembled in just a few minutes and quickly charged to become a ward. There's also so much room for creativity in making a mobile that it lends itself well to a variety of aesthetics. If you're artistic (or at least patient) you could bend and shape metal wire to make sigils, animal forms, and a decorative hoop from which to suspend everything. Beads made of minerals (i.e., "crystals") can be added to make something beautiful and potent.

Metal

Using bits of metal and/or metal objects is a traditional method of warding and safeguarding the home. It is iron, in particular, that is of the most use to the witch, as it has a long history of use protecting the home from spirits, especially the fey. It can also work to serve as an energy sink, much like a lightning rod, gathering undesired energy to it and dissipating it into the earth. Railroad spikes (collect the discarded spikes along the edges of the railroad tracks, not the spikes in use; the rustier the better) are perfect for this as they are easily driven into the ground, their tops barely noticeable amongst growing grass and plants. They can also be discreetly placed within your home, either in the corner behind doors or laid across windowsills. Two spikes crossed (to make an X not a +) and nailed above a door makes a stark but implacable ward.

The familiar old iron horseshoe is a perfect example of the use of iron as a ward. The folklore and proper means of use do vary by location, with the horseshoe being hung above a doorway points up to keep the luck in or points down. Either way, an old iron horseshoe can not only keep the luck from fleeing your household, but it can also serve as a gatekeeping ward that determines what is and is not allowed into your home (such as specifically allowing good fortune and luck within, while keeping bad luck and misfortune out).

Small square-topped nails can be substituted for railroad spikes and make for more easily hidden wards. They're perfect for binding with red string, sealing with your own fluids, and tucking atop the frame of the entrance to an apartment where it cannot be seen nor messed with, for example.

There is a lot of room for creativity and improvising in using metal. You could construct a ward using specific types of metal, based upon their planetary correspondence (not to suggest literally *forging* a ward but that, rather, one could be assembled from pieces of specific types of metal. See the *Chimes and Mobiles* section above). Scrap bits of metal, such as the cut tops of food cans, can be etched or engraved with sigils and glyphs and tucked about the home. This can be done with a rotary tool, acid, or even just a nail sharp enough to scratch the metal.

It really doesn't have to be complicated or pretty to be effective. It's the *doing* that is important. It is the making of something with your hands and breathing life into it so that it may offer practical aid and create change in your everyday life that is important. That point —making changes in one's everyday life—is one of the fundamental aims of witchcraft. While other magickal systems may concern themselves with using magick to attain godhead, witchcraft aims to make your life better. So, don't get hung up on the details. Action and doing are what make you an effective witch. Don't be a lazy witch.

Plants

Living plants are one of the most overlooked means of working magick, yet in remembering that a living plant has a sentient spirit, the incentive to work with them becomes clear. As with any relationship with a spirit, working with living plants—as opposed to dried pieces of a plant—is an active partnership. It requires a certain amount of give and take in order to maintain that relationship. You can look at the maintenance of this relationship in the terms of a contract, where you agree to provide x in exchange for y from the plant, or in the terms of a friendship, where the defined amounts of x and y are less specific and may even be disproportionate at times. In either case, if you want a spirit to do something for you then you must be prepared to do something for that spirit.

In the context of warding, working with a living plant is remarkably simple and effective. Potted plants bring the most versatility, as they can be placed in- or outdoors and relocated as needed for greater efficacy. For long-term warding, specific plants and trees can be strategically planted about the yard, serving as gatekeepers at the edges of your yard, the end of your driveway, and even the entrance to your home.

While certain types of plants do seem more appropriately suited for warding, based upon appearance and correspondence, any type of plant may be an effective ward as it is the *spirit* of the plant that will consciously be doing the hefting and guarding, rather than the warding being a causative effect due to intrinsic energetic nature of that type of plant. In fact, I've yet to find a variety of houseplant that couldn't be coaxed into at least warding its bit of window space in order to ensure that it could collect sunlight unencumbered (such as by the frequent passing through of unwanted energies) and that watering and singing to it proceeded without interruption.

Setting a living plant as a ward follows much the same as the process described in the section *Laying Your Wards* (later in this book), however, rather than charging the object, you will be conversing with the spirit of the plant: explaining what its job is and what you will do for it in exchange for its efforts. Your explanation might include exact details of its job, such as "guard this window against entrance by all spirits unknown to me; keep it shut against any energies that would negatively disrupt my and my family's lives; let naught in but that which increases our prosperity, health, and happiness."

Give an offering at this time, and make it a good one. It should be something special that not only shows how important this job is (hence the extra amazing offering) but makes it so that the plant *wants* to do the job if only to get that same type of offering again. Obviously, water is not good enough as you should already be regularly watering this plant. Rather, something special, such as a small amount of liquid fertilizer (properly diluted so as not to burn the plant's roots,) or some blood (if you menstruate, this is a perfect use for your blood; the run off blood and juices from a raw steak—as long as it's fresh—also works well). Should you give blood, make a small depression in the dirt beside the plant and pour the blood into that, then cover/fill in the depression with dirt; this helps with smells and dispersion. Depending upon the pot size, you could also bury something small and dead into the pot. A bit of a juicy raw steak, small dead fish (perhaps just part of one), small scoop of raw hamburger, or some other something that tastes of life and that can rot into the soil, feeding the plant, is also very appropriate.

Once the offering is given, explain the conditions for the plant to get such an offering again. Lay out the details of the plant's job clearly and, please, if you value your skill as a witch, please listen to what the plant says about all of this. Even a feisty transplanted stinging nettle can be coaxed into warding a room, but it requires conversation. It requires you to speak *and* listen—and to act accordingly based upon what you are told.

Plant spirits have this way about them that is almost reminiscent of children, what with the straightforwardness and need to be concise and clear with your words when talking to them. Yet they are powerful in their own right and worthy of your respect. They can do things that we are less able to easily do, as well as pull strings that, as witches, we just can't pull. They are also a very accessible type of spirit to work with, making them a good starting point if this is a new area of exploration for you. But, above all, plant spirits make magnificent allies. They are the watchers in your home when you cannot watch or see. They are teachers, whispering to you not just about the comings and goings of your other house spirits, but also whispering wisdom bundled up in riddles. You can learn much about witchcraft, the spirit world, and life by sitting in good conversation with a cherished and respected plant ally.

Powders

Powders are an interesting and frequently forgotten herb craft. Their construction and use are simple—an incense never burned, a tea or oil never steeped—yet that simplicity seems to also be why so many witches pass them by. Their sheer nature, however, makes them an effective addition to your warding regimen.

For a temporary boost to your warding efforts, sprinkling a powder across doorways (think along the top of the frame or beneath a rug), along windowsills (or even inside the window frame), and across mirrors (if they have a frame) is effective. Powders will naturally become scattered and moved, so they regularly need to be replaced and/or refreshed. For better sticking power, add a powder to a wash or mix some of your urine with the powder and then scrub your threshold. This method, mixing with your urine, is especially necessary with red brick dust in order to take advantage of its full protective power.

Dried and powdered herbs are not the only powder that is useful for warding. Eggshells and red brick dust are also useful, as is plain ol' salt.

Salt is particularly effective in warding mirrors, as it can be dissolved in water and then a thin layer of water allowed to dry on the surface of the mirror.

In using powders, the most effective powder will be the one that you grind and make yourself. Do not buy red brick dust or powdered eggshells. You are capable of drying eggshells and/or buying a brick from any hardware store (for just a few cents, too, by the way). Yes, grinding them is hard work but so what? Don't be a lazy witch, be a competent and effective witch. Be a witch who gets shit done.

Sculptures & Statuary

There are two primary ways to utilize sculptures and statuary for warding. The most basic, and most obvious, is symbolically. In this way, a sculpture will be chosen based upon its appearance and the qualities that appearance lends to protective magick. For example, a dragon figurine may be chosen due to its fierce nature and keen sight, allowing for a vigilant ward that acts quickly and gets the job done thoroughly. The figurine would be charged following a manner similar to that described below in the *Laying Your Wards* section. Admittedly, this does mean that the sculpture is essentially a charm, as discussed above, however, given the other manner in which they can be used for protection, sculptures warrant their own discussion.

Outside of a symbolic use, sculptures and statuary are frequently used within witchcraft to house spirits and, sometimes, deities. For the purpose of warding, creating a spirit (i.e., a servitor, thoughtform, elementary, etc.) and housing it in an appropriately designed sculpture can be quite effective as it can be inconspicuous while still being quite effective.

While the deliberate creation of a spirit is some serious next level magick, a protective thoughtform can be created gradually and over a period of time. This would be done through repetitive interaction with the sculpture after it has been charged and rendered a ward. Sticking with our fierce dragon sculpture example, at least once a day, in passing by the statue, you would stop and look at it. Your thoughts would focus upon the dragon, seeing it as a living creature whose sole purpose is to guard you and your family. As the days pass, this image is strengthened by the energy that you continuously feed into the sculpture. That energy accumulates, not only creating a more effective ward but eventually becoming a spirit, a thoughtform, programmed to protect that section of your home that you placed in its care.

This action of creating a thoughtform over time is an excellent warm-up to creating a servitor outright and gives you ample opportunity to practice your witchcraft every day.

Sigils & Symbols

The use of deliberately created symbols to effect change has been part of magick for longer than we've consciously recognized it as such. This process, now exemplified in the rendering of a phrase or sentence into a potent sigil, has gained greater popularity in recent years due to its efficacy and simplicity. However, that simplicity is in part deceiving, as the application of sigils and symbols proves, like most things in magick, to be fraught with complexity and greater nuance than is easily discernible.

In magick, a symbol can appear in any fashion so long as it is not a written word. Letters and words are their own sort of symbols, yes, but in magick, when we use symbols we want to tap into greater sources of power via a subconscious response. That means disengaging the logical parts of our minds and using a symbol whose meaning cannot be accurately described in words for it is felt bone deep, in blood churning heat and power. It is that subconscious response, the unintended raising of energy when seeing the symbol, that is part of the desired goal and use of symbols.

While a sigil is a type of symbol, it is distinguished by the process of its creation. That creation starts with a short sentence or phrase and then reduces it down to a collection of letters. The lines and curves of each of those letters are then rearranged to create a new symbol, filled with the power and intent of that original phrase.

To give an example, we'll go through the process of sigil creation now. The only materials needed are a blank piece of paper and a pen. For the purpose of warding, a suitable phrase to base our sigil upon could be:

sealed tight, day and night

This phrase would then be written on the paper. From there, all duplicate letters are removed from the phrase. This leaves us with:

sealdtighyn

Note that it doesn't matter if the letters are capitalized or lowercase; it's totally irrelevant. These letters are then rearranged, lines stretched and shortened, curves reversed or detached and placed along the lines of other letters altogether, angles exaggerated or obliterated entirely. The result is a symbol wholly unique to this phrase and to the one creating the sigil.

From here, the sigil must be activated. Consider this the means through which that sigil is empowered, its meaning tied to every line and imprinted upon your subconscious. To activate your sigil, you will need a piece of paper, pen, candle, and fireproof container. Draw your sigil on the new piece of paper, focus on your original phrase or sentence as you draw it. Continue to focus on that phrase, pushing it into the sigil. Now, set the paper on fire, feeding the sigil and its meaning to the flames, releasing it to the ether and sealing its meaning and form clearly within your mind. Drop the flaming paper into the fire proof container and allow it to burn to completion. Dispose of the ash by releasing them to the wind or placing in the trash.

But, how to use this potent sigil for the purpose of warding your home?

This is truly a scenario where you are limited only by your imagination.

Ways to Use Sigils to Ward Your Home

• draw the sigil on a piece of paper, fold it, and tuck it into the frame about a door or window; or simply tape the paper above the door or window

• embroider it onto the fabric of a charm bag

• draw it on paper, fold it, and place inside a charm bag

• inscribe the sigil onto candles for spells, afterward place the wax remnants into a charm bag or bury beneath the threshold of your home or the edge of your driveway

- when cleaning mirrors and windows: spray the window with cleaner then trace the sigil onto the glass, continue cleaning the glass as normal
- trace the sigil onto doorways, windows, mirrors, walls, ceilings, and floors with consecrated oil or water
- trace the sigil into your mop water prior to scrubbing the floors of your home
- trace your sigil rather than a pentacle as described in *Technique 1* in the *Emergency Warding* section below
- carve it onto a stone and hang the stone above a door or window; use the stone as part of a mobile as described above; place the stone in the pot of a plant charged with warding your home
- paint the sigil onto the backsides of mirrors, paintings, and framed photos
- paint the sigil on the bottoms of statuary
- paint the sigil onto the underside of your doormat
- draw the sigil onto pieces of masking tape, put one piece each with a sigil onto the top side of the blades of ceiling fans; every time the fan is turned on the ward is further activated and employed

The use of sigils and symbols is very flexible in application, lending itself well to other means of warding in order to boost the efficacy and coverage of that ward.

Spirits

While they themselves are not wards, spirits can serve to ward, performing that action in an active capacity, rather than the generally passive capacity of wards. The types of spirits put to this task can be plant spirits (as noted above,) thoughtforms, or even animal spirits, such as the specific spirit of a dead stag whose skull you now possess or the spirit of a snake whose rib bones you carefully gathered and cleaned. These spirits can serve not just to guard a space or doorway, but they can also serve to alert you to breaches in your other wards, as well as patrolling your home and evacuating unwanted spirit guests—even eating smaller noxious spirits and curses.

In the sculptures and statuary section above, we noted how sculpture can be used as a spirit house. Other objects, in much the same way that nearly anything can become a charm, can also be used as a spirit house. In the case of the stag spirit noted above, its skull (in your possession) would be its house, but animal spirits can also be tied to other bones from their body—such as the snake rib bones also given as an example— or even to objects and houses specially crafted for them. This can be useful as bones can become quite fragile due to improper cleaning and preservation techniques or prolonged exposure to the sun, making transferring that spirit to another vessel essential if you want to continue to keep that spirit about. In these cases, using a jar as a spirit house is convenient as you can place the crumbling, broken bone bits into the jar, for example.

Jars and bottles have a long traditional use as spirit houses, as you can fill them with appropriate things that are attractive to or belong to that spirit, your own personal effects to bind the spirit to you, and even to hold small offerings and/or bits of food and libations when feeding that spirit. Stones, as we'll go into further in just a bit, can also be used for spirit houses, but they do require some modification to change that stone from being just a stone you could find outside on the ground and into a functional spirit house.

Stones

Like many natural objects, stones are incredibly versatile within witchcraft. That they are also so easy to come by makes their use particularly recommended. When we speak of stones, it is both rocks and minerals (what are commonly and erroneously referred to as "crystals") to which we are referring as both have their uses and can even be used concurrently toward the same goal.

With both minerals and rocks, basic use (or correspondence) of that stone is determined based upon color or by what that particular stone says it is best used for—which is far more accurate and to be trusted than any correspondence list you find online or in a book. However, when it comes to warding a physical space, any stone—rock or mineral—will work, no matter its color or specific chemical makeup. Even a mineral with primarily strong healing correspondence can prove effective as a ward as its energy will, if nothing else, act as a distraction to any unwanted energy or low-level entities—serving to alter its course, neutralize that energy, or even allow for your other wards or familiar spirits to dispose of the energy or entity.

Nonetheless, to use a stone to ward against something specific, such as someone's spying, their influence (to include them hurtling magick at you), and/or specific spirits, it is better to choose a stone that better corresponds to that specific purpose. For example, a dull black stone would be well suited to absorb energy while a shiny and reflective stone would work well to distract a spying eye and a red stone would be well purposed to burn and keep out unwanted entities. You may also find it preferable to alter a stone, such as a rock common to your area, in order to render it a more potent ward. This can be done simply by carving or painting symbols onto/into the stone. Of course, you can also wrap the stone with wire, thread, or twine, and attach to it beads, metal charms, feathers, or other objects in order to create a charm as mentioned above.

To put them to use, stones can be inconspicuously tucked about your home, set beside a doorway so that the stone is hidden when the door is open, or even set in a row across a windowsill.

Constructing Your Wards

Now that you've got an idea of how simple ward construction can be, it's time to actually try your hand at making a ward, charging it, and placing it within your home. After going through the previous section, you likely already have a few things in mind that you have laying around your home or that you could quickly put together to create a ward. Cleansing those materials isn't necessary, but putting in the effort to make a ward is. Remember, the magick you work is always stronger and more effective than the magick you don't work.

It's also important to solidify everything you've read so far by putting that knowledge into practice and setting it bone deep so that it becomes reflexive (i.e., in the future, you can just get on with it rather than needing to flip back through these pages to refresh your memory). This process is also so simple that there just isn't an excuse for not creating a ward right now, regardless of where you are. On the chance that you're not at home, make the ward now, and then place it once you return home.

The example given throughout the remainder of this section is perfect for just such a situation.

Warding is also not more or less properly suited to a specific lunar phase or planetary configuration. You ward your home when you need to, when you feel compelled to, when you want to prevent problems, or when you read a how-to book on warding whose only hope is to inspire you to do the witchcraft. Please, do the witchcraft.

If you still aren't sure what materials to use, grab a small square of paper, or even a napkin, and a black pen or marker. Draw a protective symbol onto the paper. Not sure what symbol to draw? How about a simple pentacle? It is a protective symbol, after all. Or you could draw a square (representing your home) and tracing a diagonal line from corner to corner, making an X in the square (representing barred access to your home). You can always make a prettier ward later with which to replace this simple ward, although that isn't necessary. Right now, the only concern is with the actual doing of witchcraft and flexing those magickal muscles. The power is not in the aesthetic but in the doing.

As you craft your ward, keep yourself focused on its specific purpose. Just as with every spell you cast, every ward you make should have a specific purpose. Keeping that purpose in mind through the creation of the ward serves to imbue it with the appropriate energy and begin the charging process. That process of charging your ward is what transforms that piece of paper, river stone, wind chimes, or whatever you have from an ordinary everyday object into a powerful magickal device.

We've already looked at the three general things that are warded against. Keeping these in mind as guidelines, identify what it is exactly that your ward is supposed to do.

What are you in most need of guarding yourself against right now? Are you concerned about your home being broken into while you're away or sleeping? Do you have extended family members who are controlling and don't respect your boundaries? Did you get into a fight with someone on social media and now strange things are occurring at home and you're having trouble sleeping?

Having a specific focus in mind for your ward allows your ward to more effectively accomplish the job you want it to do. Remember, work specific magick for specific results. Should you require heavy warding, covering multiple foci, then lay multiple wards—each with a clear, specific focus. This creates a powerful web of protection within that space. This, too, is why having that specific function and, ideally, the location where your ward will be placed identified prior to construction will help you to work stronger and more effective magick.

Laying Your Wards: Placement & Charging

Once you've constructed your ward, charging and placing the ward should ideally take place within moments of each other. However, in the event that you've crafted a ward for someone else or you've crafted an ornate ward, perhaps even timing its construction and addition of certain specific materials per the appropriate lunar phase (as one does, at least once in their practice), it would be more effective to charge the ward and then allow it to rest on your altar, shrine, work bench, or whatever it is you call the space where you work your magick. Then, before giving the ward to its intended recipient, or just before placing your ornate ward within your home, the ward can be awakened and reminded of its task with a simple mini-charging: hold the ward in your hands, focus on its task, and then push that goal into the ward. You will feel confirmation that the ward is active and can then hand over or place the ward confidently.

As charging a ward is the final step in the construction process, knowing the specific function of the ward and where it will be placed allows you to more precisely charge the ward, making it truly potent. This also helps you to identify if you need to craft multiple wards, each charged with a different function, to lay at the same entry point.

We've already discussed what can and cannot be warded against as well as identifying what you are most in need of being protected against. Now, let's look at the most effective locations for wards within the home.

Where to Ward Your Home

In descending order of importance:

- front and back door
- windows
- doorway to/from your bedroom
- mirrors
- chimney
- doorways leading to stairs, especially if there is an actual door to close off the stairs (such as with a basement or hidden

second staircase to an attic or second floor)
- doorway to/from your bathroom and any other internal thresholds
- ceiling, floor, and walls (especially if you live in an apartment complex; the wall closest to a bothersome neighbor's house may prove especially effective and desirable)

With your first ward (or the one you're creating while you read this), ideal placement would be your front door or at the inside doorway to your bedroom, so keep this in mind as you craft your ward. If you're working with a piece of paper, you can fold the paper and slip it into any molding or trim about the doorway or secure it above the doorway.

Generally, a single ward will have a limited breadth of coverage. This is why throwing up one ward at your front door will not effectively protect you within your home. It is also why laying multiple wards throughout your home— and sometimes even at the same entry point—is strongly advised. At best, a larger and exceptionally powerful ward can cover an entire room, but bolstering with smaller wards at the entrance points will help provide stronger results and better prevent little things from slipping through. However, those little things that may slip through can be easily handled; this isn't a big deal. Your natural badass witch attitude does serve as a means of protection on its own, and this doesn't get nearly as much attention as it should. Thinking and believing that you're the baddest witch in town will have a naturally cleansing effect in your home and also serves to keep low-grade curses and the evil eye from sticking.

Additional Places to Ward Once the Inside of the Home is Secure

After the inside of your home has been sufficiently warded, there are a few places outside of your home that may also be warded for further effective protection. Note that the goal here is not to shut your home tight against the outside world—however, there may come a time when you must be on the defensive and need to protect yourself, your family, and your home to the best of your ability. This information is given to that end.

It is also important to note that, depending upon what it is that you want to ward against, it may prove more effective and preferable to ward outside your home. For example, a gossipy neighbor who doesn't respect your boundaries nor privacy would be better warded against at your property line, driveway, and the walkway to and doorway of the primary entrance they use at your home; warding the inside of your bedroom against them won't accomplish much. Common sense doesn't get thrown out just because it's magick. If that which you want to safeguard against is more effectively warded outside your home, then do so. Efficacy and results should be important concerns within your witchcraft.

Places outside your home to focus on, in no particular order:

- outsides of all doors and windows
- entrances to and all sides of any porches or balconies
- where the path to your front door meets your driveway, the sidewalk, or the road
- all entrances to your attached garage (including the vehicle entrance)

- where your driveway meets the road (this is a crossroads)
- corners of your property
- shared boundary lines with neighbors (i.e., where your property touches a neighbor's property, especially a nosy or bothersome neighbor)
- phone, computer, tablet, etc.
- *optional*: electrical outlets, sewer pipes, landline phone plugs, etc. (Personally, I think these are only ever overkill, but I know people who swear by warding these locations, additionally. For extreme situations, or when you're dealing with a mental crisis and need to take solace in a secure fortress, these extra steps may bring comfort).

Charging Your Wards

Charging is the process by which an everyday object is rendered magickally potent. Other common terms for charging include enchanting and empowering, but the process is the same regardless. Energy is gathered, focused, and pushed into the object. The object then holds that energy, that charge, gradually releasing it.

This release is both partly what makes the magick go and why it is necessary to periodically check in with your wards to see if they are dead, full (for wards whose job it is to trap), compromised, or broken and then to follow up with replacing, emptying, redoing, or fixing.

As part of the charging process, if there is a specific function of that ward (e.g., it's meant to ward against the psychic influence of another witch you got into a fight with on social media) that function would be programmed into the ward during the charging. This is simply a matter of holding that function in your mind and pushing it into the ward. There are no other tools needed but your ability to focus and send energy in order to charge any object. No candles, no incense, just you and the skill you've cultivated and honed to shape and move energy.

It is necessary to note that charging and consecrating are not the same thing. These two processes accomplish fundamentally different ends, though the similarity in potency and use of an object that has undergone either process naturally means that these two processes are often conflated. To consecrate means to make something sacred. It involves the presence and power of deities to transform that object, taking the onus of action off of the witch and placing it upon the Gods. Often times, this process of consecration is done solely to transform an object into something sacred *for the Gods*, but it is commonly used now to mean delineating that object's use and purpose to one specific thing.

Either way, wards are not consecrated. When you charge a ward, you are using *your* skill alone to transform it and make it powerful. Making and laying a ward is not something that requires the presence nor power of any deity and most deities appreciate your ability to handle things on your own. Witchcraft is a craft that works without or without the involvement of deities but it cannot work without your effort to develop and hone your magickal skills.

A Final Note Before You Lay Your Wards

While physically cleaning your home isn't warding in itself, it is definitely a form of protection magick as it's hard for things to stick when there's nothing to which they may stick. A clean, organized house has no places for things to hide. Deep physical cleaning can be done before or after warding is in place, it makes no difference efficacy wise. However, cleaning beforehand means you don't have to clean around your wards. Personally, I prefer beforehand as the physical cleaning can be rendered a psychic cleansing, leaving you with easier work.

Emergency Warding: When You Have no Tools & Need to Ward Now

At some point in your practice, it won't be unusual to find yourself in need of immediate warding. Something will be going on that necessitates strong protection magick yet not only is there not enough time to construct a ward but doing so simply isn't practical. You may find yourself under emotional stress, be experiencing a panic attack, there are suddenly a number of odd and inexplicable occurrences in your home (e.g., doors opening and/or closing on their own, loud bumps and banging sounds, objects falling off of walls and/or counters, etc.), or you simply have an overwhelming sensation that you need an extra bit of protection *right now*.

The following techniques are useful in these situations as they are simple to do, effective, and will provide you with a temporary boost of protection. Keep in mind that the duration of protection these techniques afford tends to only last for a handful of hours as there is nothing physically present to anchor or replenish the energy.

These techniques are purely energetic. As such, if you are not proficient in projecting energy without any tools or objects nor in being able to sense energy you project by either feeling and/or seeing it, these may or may not actually work for you. Magick does not work through good intentions and well wishes. Its effective use requires the development and honing of skill: skill brings results and successfully wrought magick. Do the work, get the results. There are no shortcuts or quick fixes.

Technique #1

This technique can be used any time additional warding is needed and it works especially well when used in conjunction with physical wards. It is also very simple and can be used as an energetic exercise to help build and strengthen ability, even with small children. It is useful for providing extra security to doorways, windows, and mirrors and, thus, makes a great addition to a nightly routine for yourself and/or any children you may have. Even if you do no other energetic exercises, this technique done consistently (i.e., at least a few times each week for a sustained period of time, such as several months) will dramatically increase your ability to directly manipulate and sense energy—skills that are fundamental to all systems of magick, including witchcraft.

Essentially, you will be projecting energy through your dominant hand, tracing a banishing pentacle onto the surface of a closed door or into the open doorway, or onto a window or mirror. You do not need to physically touch the door, window, or mirror and you can effectively lay the pentacle onto the door, window, or mirror from several feet away. Until you are more comfortable and experienced with this technique, standing no more than an arm's length away and facing the place you will be laying the pentacle directly (rather than at an angle) will make it easier to send the energy and sense (see and/or feel) the pentacle.

Note that a banishing pentacle is laid by moving your hand in a counterclockwise motion. However, the pentacle must appear to be banishing (versus an invoking/evoking pentacle) from the perspective of that which is being warded against. To put that more clearly, if you are standing within your child's bedroom and are going to ward their window, you would begin at the top point of the star and move your hand down and to the right, completing the star and then moving your hand down and to the right, again, to complete the circle about it. From within the room, this would appear to be an *invoking* pentacle, however, as you are barring entrance through the window to things *outside* the room, the pentacle does appear to be banishing from *that* perspective. But, if once leaving your child's room you were going to lay a ward at the doorway, you would begin at the top and move your hand down and to the *left*, moving counterclockwise through the star and circle about it. This is because you are now outside of the room and sealing the doorway against things that are outside, as well.

These energetic pentacles will naturally dissipate within several hours, though you may find them still intact when you wake in the morning if you laid them before bed.

Technique #2

Much like the last technique, this will feel familiar to anyone who has participated in a ritual based upon Wiccan ritual structure. For this technique, you will perform the same action as you would when casting a circle: projecting energy from your dominant hand to create a barrier. The difference here is that you will walk the perimeter of your home or bedroom (depending upon the situation), projecting the energy along the line of the wall.

Begin at the main entrance of your home (or bedroom) and walk clockwise, following the wall. If you are walking through your home, you will naturally go in and out of rooms and closets. As you walk, you can employ the first technique, listed above, laying a banishing pentacle at every doorway, at every window, and upon every mirror you pass. Continue to follow the wall until you return to where you started.

This energetic barrier will temporarily bolster your wards or serve in their stead to provide you with an extra level of protection. In combination, these two techniques will both help to strengthen your ability to move and sense energy—skills that you will find invaluable in your practice as a witch.

While neither of these techniques requires the use of tools, they can be enhanced through the use of chants or incantations. Words can be potent vehicles for power and can help you to better focus should you be using these techniques in a time of emergency or stress. It is advised that you craft your own words of power to use, as they will naturally be stronger for you. Should you find yourself lacking poetic skill, I offer the following chant for your use. It is especially well suited should you be laying an energetic barrier as detailed in the second technique.

As is a circle a sacred space,
so is this home a protected place.
Wards on the ceiling,
wards on the floor,
wards on the windows,
wards on the floor.
Bound by love, for that's what it contains,
and nothing else within it remains.

Afterword

Throughout this book, there has been one point stressed above all others: the importance of action. Witchcraft is about what you are doing. It does not matter how many pretty candles you own, how many bones are scattered about your work space, how many exotic herbs fill your cupboards, nor how many books you've read.

You become a better witch because of everything that you've done and everything you are doing. It is that action, that building of skill and that amassing of experience that makes the doing of magick reflexive, that tends that knowledge into true wisdom.

It is my sincerest hope that this book inspires you to act, to make fewer excuses why you can't, and to do the witchcraft. I hope that it encourages you to rely more strongly on yourself rather than having the "right tools" or the "right timing." Don't worry that your wards aren't pretty, dirty, sparkly, rotting, bright, dark, vibrant, or dead enough. Forget about the aesthetic, **do the witchcraft**.

Glossary

altar purposely constructed temporary physical space that serves as a portal between the worlds through which energies and entities may be called forth or sent through; a flat surface on which is deliberately arranged particular religious/spiritual tools and objects for the effect of their combined energies and the way that effect contributes to achieving a defined goal; contrast with *shrine*

bless a religio-spiritual technique in which the grace, favor, attention, and/or energy of a deity is called forth upon a person, place, object, endeavor, or situation; originally referred to a religious rite in which an object or person was consecrated by marking with blood

charge to consciously infuse an object with energy as well as align its inherent energy to a specific goal; similar terms include *enchant* and *empower*

charm an object that is deliberately constructed (or modified) and charged so as to perform a magickal function; originally meaning an incantation, song, or verse that was recited as a spell, as a term in contemporary witchcraft, it may refer to a magickally charged object or spoken magick

cleanse a magico-religious technique for removing excess and/or unwanted energy from an object or place so that energy will not interfere with further magickal work or day to day events in that location

consecrate a ritual technique wherein an object or place is made sacred and set apart from everyday use by being dedicated to use for one or more deities

counter-curse a ritual technique used to counter the effects—intended or actual—of a curse by redirecting the curse back at the sender; although it is a defensive action, counter-cursing is subject to the same ethical discretion as cursing

crossroads any intersection of two or more pathways, including roads, trails, and walkways (i.e., the location where the walkway to your front door meets the sidewalk is a crossroads, the location where the doorway to your bedroom meets the hallway is a crossroads)

curse a spell cast for the purpose of causing harm, pain, or other forms of discomfort to someone; curses are typically done in retaliation for wrongdoings for which there exists no other form of recourse

deity a type of spirit with considerable power and influence over the physical world, Their distinction as "gods" may be due to status (through our honor and worship, we have elevated Them to that place of power and rank) or a trait intrinsic to Their nature; some deities were originally land spirits or even human before becoming a god

evil eye a curse cast through a look, stare, or gaze; similar term is being *overlooked*

godhead the quality of divinity, divine nature, that which makes a god a god

intention the desired outcome of a spell or other act of magick; intention alone is not magick, is not a spell, and is not capable of accomplishing change; intention that is not supported through appropriate action—magickal or otherwise—is little more than thoughts and wishes

magick the action of utilizing spiritual forces to create change; many different systems and approaches exist, witchcraft is one such system; magickal actions include things such as spells, rituals, divination, spirit communication, astral travel, and more

magickal hygiene spiritual techniques used to maintain and promote energetic health; it is a preventative measure

Paganism a contemporary religious movement that is an umbrella for many contemporary religions and religious traditions, these traditions are largely polytheistic and animistic, many are an attempt to revive the indigenous religions of Europe and the surrounding area

psychic a catch all descriptor for energetic and/ or spiritual forces and/or skills, e.g., the ability to feel and manipulate energy is a psychic skill as is intuition

servitor a spirit who is deliberately and consciously created through magickal ritual for the purpose of fulfilling a task as designated by the person who created them, that task can be to guard a location or to retrieve information, for example

shrine dedicated physical space that has been devoted to that particular deity; a flat surface upon which items have been placed for the delight of a deity and to aid in the worship of that deity; unlike an altar, a shrine is a permanent space; an altar that is not taken down is more appropriately called a shrine when not in use

sigil a symbol distinguished through the process of its creation and use for magick; a sigil is created by rendering a brief phrase or word (that sums up its intended use) to only non-repeated letters and then arranging the shapes of those letters into a symbol that captures the essence of that phrase/word for the creator of the sigil

spell a concentrated and deliberate ritual act of magick for the purpose of creating specific change; a spell utilizes spiritual forces to create measurable changes in the energy within and without a situation and/or person

spirit any being that exists on a spectrum of energetic beings, some of these beings may have once been physically incarnate—such as spirits of deceased humans & animals—while others may have never been physically incarnate—such as some (but not all) spirits of place (the genius loci), familiars, the Good Folk, and the Gods

thoughtform a created spirit; unlike servitors, thoughtforms can be and often are created unintentionally, they generally lack specificity of purpose and frequently appear to do little more than exist and lightly interact with living humans; thoughtforms can be and sometimes are mistaken for other spirits, such as genius loci, spirits of the deceased, and even gods

ward a physical object used as an anchor point for energy for the purpose of providing magickal protection and spiritual defense; to ward is to enact any sort of semi-permanent magickal defense for a place or living person

Wicca a contemporary witchcraft religion founded by Gerald Gardner in the 1940's; its popularity is responsible, in part, for the advancement of modern Paganism as it has, in recent years, largely served as a "gateway religion" to other religions and traditions within the Pagan movement

witchcraft one of many magickal systems, distinct in its strong focus on creating change within the everyday, and defined by its fundamental inclusion of animism, divination, the land, ritual, and spirit work; it is not inherently religious but can be melded within a variety of religious contexts or practiced wholly without

zoological remains the organic bodily remains of animals; zoological remains are used in witchcraft for their inherent liminality, aiding us in tapping into power and serving as a bridge between the worlds that witch and spirit alike can traverse

Index

A

altar, 2, 71
awareness, 26, 27, 39

B

blessing, unwanted, 14-15
bodily fluids, 46
    blood, 38, 50, 56
    urine, 38, 39, 40, 52
bones, 41, 42, 44, 60, 61, 89
bottles, 38, 61

C

charge, 25, 36, 37, 42, 43, 44, 53, 54, 59, 71,
    72, 76, 77, 78
charms, 36-42, 54, 60, 63
    herbal charm bags, 41-42, 58
cleaning, 59, 61, 78-79
cleansing, 1, 2, 8, 11, 20, 40, 65, 74, 79
consecrating, 77
crossroads, 8, 12, 76
curses, 2, 7, 8, 14, 38, 60, 74
    counter-curse, 38, 40

D

E

F

G

H

I

J

M

N

P

S

T

thread, 40, 41, 63

tools, 37, 46, 77, 81, 82, 86, 89

W

Z

About Althaea Sebastiani

Althaea Sebastiani is a spirit worker, author, and spirit-led witch with 25 years' experience. Her practice is land-based and devotional, focused on being responsive to the spirits of the land wherever her travels take her and doing right by the Gods Who have called her into Their service. When not writing or cavorting with Gods and spirits, Althaea spends her time wrangling six half-feral children with her husband, wandering about the West in a tiny traveling house, and living off-grid in the wilderness.

Find her on social media @LadyAlthaea or at www.ladyalthaea.com, where you can find her other titles as well as her available courses in witchcraft and Paganism.

Made in the USA
Columbia, SC
06 June 2023

17674460R00072